# ECO ECO
## Ecological Economics

# ECO ECO
## Ecological Economics

*Jane Robertson and John Robertson*

THE CHOIR PRESS

First published in the United Kingdom in 2019 by
The Choir Press

ISBN 978-1-78963-078-7

# CONTENTS

———

# Introduction

*Ecology*: the branch of biology which deals with the relations of organisms to one another and to their surroundings.

*Economics*: the practical and theoretical science of the production and distribution of wealth.

The words *ecology* and *economics* share a common root: the Greek word *oikos*, meaning a house.

Ecology is the way the natural world manages its house.

Economics is the way society manages its house.

The contentions of this book are that the natural world is the best guide to our economic activities, that supply and demand are insufficient determinants, that profit and loss are not alternatives, that wealth cannot be created but can be lost. *Ecological economics* is a term that has been coined to encapsulate these ideas.

Let's begin with our definition of economics; it's not the only one, but it contains some debatable points.

Economics is the practical and theoretical science of the production and distribution of wealth.

First, the production of wealth. The only wealth we have comes from the earth and the lifeforms of the earth, the force of gravity, the electromagnetic forces, and the energy of the sun (energy is the ability to do work). We cannot produce any of this. When we talk about 'producing wealth' we mean making profit.

The First Law of Thermodynamics tells us that energy can be converted from one form to another. It cannot be created or destroyed; it can, however, be wasted. In any energy conversion some energy is wasted: not destroyed, but put beyond use. In the science of thermodynamics the energy that is so wasted is called *entropy*. So it is with wealth.

Wealth cannot be produced; it can be converted from one form to another, and it can be wasted. When we talk about wealth production, what we are describing is the conversion or combination of raw materials to make a more marketable form; that is, a form considered more useful or desirable in the eyes of the potential customer. We might say we are adding value, and when we realise that value we make a profit. So when we talk about the production of wealth we mean making profit.

When we introduce the notion of profit, we already have the notion of distribution of wealth. In making a profit we move wealth from its original owner to a new owner, from the owners of raw material to the owners of finished product, and so bring about a distribution of wealth. Profit implies a flow of wealth in one direction, while, from the same standpoint, a flow in the opposite direction would be seen as a loss. Profit and loss are not alternatives; to fill the glass I must empty the bottle. As wealth cannot be created, one man's profit must be funded by another's loss. Profit and loss is a zero-sum game but inevitably means inequity between the partners. This inequity and the accumulation of wealth is the concern of welfare economics, a difficult and subjective business to which we'll return shortly.

Another look at the economic model of supplier of raw materials to producer of finished goods, resulting in profit, shows that it is not cyclic; the finished goods do not (intentionally, anyway) augment the stock of raw materials. Contrast the natural system. Growth may be seen as analogous to the production of wealth, but growth is inevitably followed by decay; ashes to ashes, dust to dust. The product of growth returns as the resource of new growth. Nowadays we call it recycling. The effectiveness with which the natural system does this is the key to its persistence.

The natural system has no ultimate ambition to accumulate wealth; 'sceptre and crown must tumble down and in the dust be equal laid with the poor crooked scythe and spade' (Shirley, 1659). The trouble with economics is that it is not generally able to achieve this level of impartiality.

Economic growth is defined as the growth of the real output (goods and services produced from factor inputs) of an economy over time, normally measured as increase in GDP. A high rate of growth is one of the four main objectives of macroeconomic policy. Economic growth is seen as desirable because, if there are more consumer goods to buy, more profit can be made and more social services provided, all this resulting in improved living standards. In other words, increasing supply drags up consumption (demand) and increases profits, and some of that profit can be returned in wages and, through taxation, can fund the provision of social services.

Since profit entails loss, in time profit will diminish, as a result of scarcity of raw materials or increasing raw material costs (and most likely both), and the rate of growth will fall off until there is no growth. Ultimately growth is unsustainable; just as in the natural system, growth is inevitably followed by decay. We have to find another way to keep the wheel turning, and the best way may be to follow the natural world's precedent: recycle and reuse.

The definition of economics given above is not the only one and can now be extended. Economics is the study of the problem of using available factors of production as efficiently as possible so as to attain the maximum fulfilment of society's unlimited demand for goods and services. Economics has a micro and a macro dimension. Microeconomics is concerned with the efficient supply of particular products. Macroeconomics is concerned with the overall efficiency of resource use in the economy. Efficiency is the relationship between inputs (factors of production) and outputs (goods and services). Measured in physical terms it's called technological efficiency; measured in cost terms it's economic efficiency.

Technological efficiency seeks to determine the best possible combination of factor inputs (factors of production) to produce a given level of output. Economic efficiency seeks to identify that combination of factor inputs which minimises the cost of producing a given level of output.

In the short term, minimising the cost (of inputs) may maximise the profit, but it would nonetheless deplete the resource. Seeking minimum cost does not mean we know the true cost. We are guided by our sense of what value the market might place on our finished product and what profit we might make. The truth is we may not be able to determine the true cost; we may not even be aware of what the true cost comprises. There may be concomitant costs of which we are ignorant or heedless. We may while depleting our resources be putting them effectively beyond reach, reducing our ability to do useful work, wasting wealth, in thermodynamic terms increasing entropy in our economic system. Contrast the natural system, where the emphasis is on minimising entropy by recycling and renewing. There is already a growing, alarmingly so, body of evidence that we are polluting, destroying, poisoning our environment. Supply and demand are no longer sufficient determinants of economic activity.

Welfare economics is a branch of economics that is concerned with the way economic activity ought to be arranged so as to maximise economic welfare.

Unfortunately there may be as many views on this outcome as there are people, and workers in this field have sought welfare criteria which avoid interpersonal comparisons. Despite the difficulties, such efforts are increasingly important.

There's a new imperative on the block. It's generally referred to by the umbrella title of *climate change* and, it seems, it favours no one, and no one is proof against it. In it economists should find what they have been seeking: welfare criteria free of interpersonal comparisons. The evidence of its existence seems to be present. It seems to be getting worse. It may be due to increasing emissions of 'greenhouse' gases into the atmosphere. It may be due to changes in land use or population growth. It seems to be happening faster than the natural world can adjust.

The one law which seems to apply in everything we do is the Law of Unintended Consequences. We can't assume that we appreciate all the knock-on effects of our actions, nor that it's safe or even reasonable to leave it to the 'experts'. Of course governments can and do influence economic activity. What can all of us do? As consumers we control to a great extent the demand side of the economy. We need to bring a third factor to our supply and demand model: survival. Our demands now need to be governed by their effect on our continued survival.

# Chapter I

*Ecological Economics*

It is well known that we cannot continue as we are if we care about the planet. So many books have been written on the subject of the need for change. This book concentrates on the subject of economics and begins to chart a new course of action.

Economics has always been about growth and how to make a profit. Profit can only be made by exploiting the planet. We remove raw materials like iron, copper or tin – in short, non-renewable resources – from the earth in order to fashion these into artefacts that people wish to buy. The earth has many scars on its surface made by removing raw materials which cannot be replaced, and so eventually the whole world is poorer for all this activity. The earth suffers the loss, the second part of the philosophy of profit and loss. The earth is a non-renewable resource. A growing economy has always implied that we need more and more non-renewables, and if these resources are finite then they must also be shrinking. These precious resources are irreplaceable.

Profit and loss can no longer be the long-term direction of economics. In fact the word *economics* rather describes the opposite of profit and loss: it derives from *economy*, which is about prudent stewardship, the careful use of resources. Someone who is economical is someone who is careful and uses available resources in a considered way: just the opposite of our application of economics, which has become exploitative and to do with profit and loss to the exclusion of all else. It builds in obsolescence, because it needs consumerism to thrive. When the product is broken it is thrown away and we are left with mountains of white goods and rubbish. A dystopic society.

## Products for Life

In contrast we could build things to last, and to be easy to repair when they break down, making it simple to access the workings of the machine and to acquire parts. We could create a whole new industry using people's talents and experience to repair, renew and reuse goods when they are damaged or broken. All this could be done with the co-operation of the manufacturers, who could improve the product to make it last a lifetime. If manufacturers provided this service they would not have to engage in built-in obsolescence and heedless innovation to stay in business and would, at the same time, conserve irreplaceable resources.

This is a new ecological economics where we use words to say what they really mean. This begins to look like a model based on natural ecological systems. We have to replace built-in obsolescence, which is exploitative, with ecological systems which reflect the natural world. The natural world is conservative. In nature the waste systems which produce carbon dioxide manufacture a product necessary for trees, which in turn transmute carbon dioxide back into oxygen, a product necessary for us. We need a cyclical economics that reflects ecology, not an exploitative growth economics which needs more consumers and a growing population. We need to apply ecological economics to travel, manufacture, gadgets, building homes, recreation and all the activities we enjoy to make a life worthwhile. Most of all, we need to have a society which cares more for its people. Not only must the products have a lifetime of usefulness, but people need the same consideration too. Then we can all be a part of this considerable exercise which cares about the planet and everything and everyone in it.

Between 1970 and today the population of the earth has doubled and the global economy has quadrupled. Growth is no longer an option. We have to stabilise every aspect of our living so that the planet can survive and we can all benefit. We have to take growth out of the equation.

A manufacturer who maximises growth and profits to the exclusion of all else will show little enthusiasm for goods which will last a lifetime. The employees of such a company will be a part of the process, units to be made redundant and replaced by robots if at all possible. Robots can use scarce materials many times faster than people. A company with many robots will have only a few employees; to make a profit they have to be kept to a minimum. We can only be consumers when we are employed and, unfortunately for the manufacturers, robots do not need washing machines. This system fails people and is not sustainable. People need to be part of an inclusive, regenerative system.

There was a time when people worked from home in a cottage industry. They used their talents to weave cloth, for example. They found suitable dyes and made a good product, but modern industry looks for economies of scale. We decanted all these self-sufficient artisans into factories, which were often dirty and dangerous. We cared little about where or how they lived. Now labour is considered expensive and, because tasks have been simplified, a robot can do the boring jobs just as well. People are therefore redundant and removed.

On the other hand Cadbury was created by concerned individuals who cared for their employees. They created villages and retirement homes for their workforce because the people mattered to them; a company which made a good product also fitted the model of ecological economics where product and people matter. A good brand should be successful when its manufacture involves a good future for its employees. These are the companies which we can choose to support.

When we purchase a brand we also purchase a way of life. Everything has to be taken into consideration, from the cocoa bean to the final product. The choices we make when even just buying chocolate matter if we are to save the planet and make life successful and pleasant for everyone.

## Capitalism

Between 1970 and today 60% of all vertebrate life has disappeared. This is disconcerting; we too are vertebrates. We also need the climate to be within very specific limits of temperature and humidity to survive. The immigration we in the temperate zone are experiencing may well be due to climate change; temperatures above 40°C are impossible for us to live with because this is above our blood temperature of 36.8°C.

Capitalism requires growth to succeed. Growth is the main ambition of all entrepreneurs who wish to accumulate capital. To feed growth we also have to encourage consumerism and immigration. Capitalism forces its own agenda on us all. Capitalism is the status quo and this philosophy is the all-pervasive enduring model. It depends on vast inputs of money and resources, putting pressure on companies to win contracts by any means; as has been shown with the largest companies, they become Ponzi schemes relying on input of capital to sustain an endeavour running out of ideas. Any default of the input, especially cash, can cause them to fail and go bankrupt. The company would do better to put money aside for a rainy day, but all profits are harvested for salaries at the top; little is put into pension funds or returned to the makers of wealth, the employees.

There is little to reduce the suffering of the many when companies fail. Large companies are always in danger of collapsing like a pack of cards.

## The Consumer Is in Control

When electricity was first produced, government policies encouraged people to use it and buy the latest gadgets. Internet shopping satisfies consumer demand. Consumerism is easy. You can purchase anything at the touch of a button. This results in a free-for-all rush to consume, with little thought between the perceived need to buy and the press of a button. Consumers are encouraged to purchase the latest gadget, the new thing, and to believe that life is better if they have the latest technology. It becomes a must-have competition. The introduction to the technology programme *Click* says it all: the old has to be smashed and thrown away to make way for the latest gadget and grow rubbish tips. Technology is not the problem; it is the lack of consideration given to this thoughtless attitude that ensures that we are inevitably moving towards dystopia. We need technology to save the planet, not just to entertain.

The wonderful thing is that it is consumers who are in control. We can move towards dystopia and a collapsing planet, or we can work out how to help the planet survive in the face of all this consumer choice. We can pause when presented with a new purchase to consider very carefully whether we need it at all.

The company which uses renewable resources

intelligently to improve life should get our vote and prosper, while the company pursuing an obsolescent capitalism should not and will fail. The population as a whole is concerned about the environment and pollution, and it would help the planet if we could support endeavours which are ecologically thoughtful. We have to reduce built-in obsolescence and mass production by robots and increase manufacturing for life. We have to consider the lifetime of the product and its reuse when it is eventually unwanted, and the treatment of people.

## Renewable Energy

It is time to put technology to use finding ways to develop a new ecological economics. There should be no waste. Waste must become the new resource. We should refrain from removing raw materials from the planet whenever possible and should especially not extract them to make a profit. The capitalist's profit is the planet's loss. To save the planet, capitalism has to be replaced with ecological economics, and consumers are in control.

Every country has raw materials which can be mined, and in many of these countries conditions are becoming unendurable due to climate change. Consideration must be given to the negative effects on the immediate environment, and also on the world's climate, of extracting quantities of raw materials and moving them around the globe to resource manufacturing. Countries like Australia which are experiencing the adverse effects of climate change and temperatures in excess of 40°C could reduce the sale of raw materials to make industry think of recycling more and force the adoption of ecological economics.

We have learned that coal causes pollution, and so we limit the extraction and use of coal. We are using technology to find other ways to make electricity. Wind power, solar energy, and water-generated electricity are the most common forms of so-called 'renewable energy'. We could build many tidal lagoons like the one proposed at Swansea providing on-shore electricity. Projects like this sited around the UK could provide as much electricity as a nuclear power station. These schemes have other benefits too, stopping coastal erosion and protecting vulnerable areas from flooding. They could provide electricity for a lifetime and offer work for the local community and engineers, especially if the turbines were made in Britain. The Swansea turbine scheme is clever because it generates electricity on the ebb and the flow.

Nuclear power stations are costly to build and maintain, and very costly to decommission, and all these problems have to be taken into consideration. No satisfactory solution has been found for the disposal of nuclear waste. People have to be kept away from nuclear sites indefinitely; they are not at all people-friendly. We must be ever mindful of the effects that could result from climate change; sited on the coast, nuclear power stations are vulnerable to any variation in sea level, which can no longer be taken for granted.

# CHAPTER II

---

In the last sixty years environmental pollution has increased by 30%. You just have to visit a city to sense that all is not well. We have to consider a new ecological economics.

## Prefabricated Houses

After World War II we had to build houses rapidly because many people were homeless. We did this by building prefabricated houses. Today we could improve the structure of such homes and we could use the most obvious resource available: wood. These homes could be insulated with wool or plastic waste that has been reformed into sheeting. Now solar energy panels could be fitted to each one so that the occupants do not have to choose between eating and heating. Each house could have an area of garden so that there is space for the growing of flowers, vegetables, and trees to absorb more carbon dioxide and improve the atmosphere. Prefabricated timber houses could be made to last a lifetime. They would be easy to repair and maintain. Furthermore they could be built in sections in a large vacated shop, like Homebase, out of town in a shopping precinct. Large stores which have closed down could be replaced with new ecological industries.

Of course timber has to be delivered to a factory and sections transported to site. This has to be given consideration. Prefabricating plants could be sited near tree plantations, then out-of-town sites could be used for warehousing and distribution.

Building prefabricated houses means that dwellings could be situated close to factories so that employees do not have far to travel. Where forest management is necessary, prefabricated homes could be built near the workplace all over the country to increase the housing stock.

## White Goods

White goods could be restored in vacated premises for reuse, in co-operation with an enlightened manufacturer. Perhaps the manufacturer of the product could expand the business into repairing and renewing the product with a collection and delivery service including plumbing and installation: a one-stop shop. This would create a lifetime of work for employees as well as a product for life. There are endless opportunities for entrepreneurs to get involved with renewal and repair in town centres so that all domestic appliances last a lifetime. Domestic appliances could be purchased from repairers and manufacturers to keep all these white goods and their precious materials away from rubbish heaps. Of course, until the new economics is established, discarded appliances could be reprocessed to replenish the steel supply. This is important for our wellbeing too. We have to control manufactur-ng and rubbish to control pollution. The consumer is in control and can encourage the good to replace the wasteful.

Ecological economics provides a new model. Sensible wages have to be paid to all employees so that the wealth of a company is distributed across the workforce in an equable way.

## The Fashion Industry

Fashionable fabrics can be made from renewable resources like cotton or wool or silk, but there are environmental costs. The fashion industry causes more pollution than aviation and shipping combined. The mass market in cheap throwaway clothes treats people as renewable resources to be exploited and abuses the planet's resources. The growers and the manufacturers make profits while the planet and people suffer. Cotton needs water in large amounts and only grows in hot climates where water is a precious resource. Any renewable resource can become a scarce resource if we do not use it in moderation.

The consumer can help to reduce the damage to the environment. It would help the planet to recover if we bought clothes to last and took appropriate care of them. The garment industry could have a different emphasis: not cheap and soon rejected to keep up with the latest fashion, but sensible, enduring, and smart, to last and save the planet.

Everyone is really keen to do something to save the planet, and what we consume will make a difference. Things are going so badly wrong. Unfortunately litter picking and clearing rubbish from beaches is tackling the problem from the wrong end. There should be no need to throw away anything which is still functional.

Since 1960 environmental pollution has increased by 30%. This is a crisis caused by humans, and if we are careful and thoughtful about our purchasing then we can reduce pollution and the demand for scarce resources. We are encouraged to consume, whether we need to update our possessions or not. It is fashionable to be able to consume in every field, whether cars or clothes, because the choice is there, not because it is necessary. We can get into the ridiculous situation where we encourage technology to change so much that all our records and data need to be re-stored using the latest technology if we are to continue to access them. It will soon be easier to read the Rosetta Stone than to retrieve our own immediate past.

We should endeavour to make our purchases last as long as possible. We have to reduce our purchasing to reduce pollution, and on this we can exercise control.


*Fireworks*

On Guy Fawkes Night and New Year's Day and whenever possible we celebrate by setting off tons of fireworks. We do not need to celebrate in this way, but we have to have the biggest and best display of all the displays around the world, and hundreds of tons of fireworks are set off for our entertainment. Just think how marvellous it would be if Britain set a precedent and did not use fireworks at all in order to save the planet. We could begin to improve an atmosphere already saturated with smoke and fumes. Setting off fireworks is a tradition, it is what is done, but do we have to compete in this nonsensical, detrimental way? Fireworks are not good for the environment and should not be for pleasure. This sort of activity may shorten some people's lives and should not be seen as entertainment for the many.

# CHAPTER III

---

*The Food Industry*

Some 60% of British food is home-grown. Perhaps we could try to grow 100% of our food and have some to export, because half the world is starving.

It is quite ridiculous that both farmers and fishermen should have to throw away a large part of their produce because it is deemed not to be acceptable. Perhaps it is not the right size or it's over a set quota. It is unforgivable to waste food at all. So much food is wasted that if we used all of the harvest this alone would provide for 100% of our needs. This is the basis of our nation's wealth. Even small, badly shaped vegetables could be chopped up and either tinned or frozen.

The climate in our country is perfect for farming, and as you travel across the country you can see that the countryside is put to good use. Farmers continually develop and diversify in order to produce more and better crops. We need colleges to supply apprentices to assist in the farming industry so that farmers are not short of help and so that farmers can pass on good practice to the next generation. The fruit industry is also impressive, and enthusiastic apprentices could help here and in associated industries. Colleges could encourage all young people who love the countryside to find employment in an industry which uses renewable resources and which is the basis of the nation's wealth and health. In schools children used to be taught how to cook so that when older they could put all this wonderful produce to good use. Today children can leave school not knowing how to boil an egg. We should get our priorities right.

A milk marketing board could, with the help of all farmers, establish a price for the product which would enable our dairy farmers to thrive. A board of agriculture could co-ordinate farming so that all produce is used throughout the country and none is wasted.

Just recently it has been said that animals pollute the environment because they produce carbon dioxide and methane and that therefore their numbers should be reduced, but all animals are necessary in the food chain. Some crops put nitrogen into the soil and crop rotation could help to reduce the need for fertilisers, but all animals nourish and enrich the soil. It is more urgent to reduce carbon dioxide and pollution caused by cars and aviation than to reduce the animal population. British meat is a wholesome product and every diet has to include protein. We cannot all switch to soya beans and chickpeas without looking at the food chain as a whole. Where are these peas and beans being grown and is the Amazon forest being removed for their production?

It is impossible to feed a growing population

indefinitely. It would be better if the population in our country could stabilise so that we could attempt to feed and house everyone. The industrialists and those who grow capital need the population to grow in order to encourage more consumerism. There is a contradiction here! We cannot have an increase in population and at the same time reduce the food supply.

## Genetic Engineering of Crops

It's in no one's interest to engineer crops which are sterile so that seed can only be purchased from one supplier, but this does not mean that genetic engineering of crops has no place in agriculture. Genetic engineering has in fact been practised for thousands of years by selective breeding.

Genetic engineering may be needed in the face of climate change; the land could become too dry or too wet to produce today's crops. Farmers have to have a diversity of seeds available to cope with a changing climate and to maximise growth. Potato famines are less likely to happen if, for example, we develop a potato resistant to blight and moulds whilst encouraging insects which are needed for pollination. Genetic engineering can produce larger and even more nutritious crops. Monocultures are very vulnerable and diversity is necessary for our survival.

Horticulture also uses renewable resources. Flowers encourage insects which are essential for pollination and the growing of crops. Gardens provide a green belt in cities. Beekeepers are important because they care about the health of bees and produce honey, another renewable resource.

## Growing Food in Cities

Hydroponics could be a source of food in cities where there is a suitable vacant warehouse looking for a successful alternative venture. Hydroponics is a system of growing vegetables in recirculating water to produce lettuce and leeks, for example, all year round. One benefit of hydroponics is that the product can be produced closer to the customer, reducing transport needs. Of course rhubarb and mushrooms can be grown in warehouses too, where the environment can be controlled. The more food can be produced near the population, the better.

## Fishing

Perhaps we will soon get control of our coastal fishing waters and watch the fishing ports thrive once again. We will be able to catch a variety of species of fish and bring home all the different types to be sorted in the market. Most of the fish caught will be edible and, although the consumer enjoys cod and haddock, there are many other white fish that could be enjoyed too. We should not overfish the seas around us, but this will be ours to control. No fish should be thrown away when the whole catch can be utilised.

Perhaps we could once again link up fishing ports

with food processors and markets by rail to enable food to arrive fresh at its destination. Not long ago boat builders could be seen working on the shore making boats for the fishing industry. These talented craftsmen might well reappear when the fishing industry revives and thrives again. All these skills should be revived and encouraged so that young people have a diversity of occupations to look forward to as they leave education, because people matter. We must grow diversity in education and the workplace and make use of all our talents.

It is so important to look at the good use of all resources, both renewable and non-renewable. We may need to use non-renewable resources, but we must use them sparingly and thoughtfully, never forgetting that they are not replaceable. If we could consume in moderation then the planet would respond.

The earth may have a number of stable conditions, but it almost certainly has only one that would favour us, and we must control our exploitative instincts and achieve that outcome if we can.

## *Windmills*

We now have a major industry producing energy from windmills, yet we have not developed this resource in such a way that we use all the electricity produced. When not required to supply the grid windmills could be used to charge batteries so that energy can be stored. The power of windmills could be used to electrolyse water, producing hydrogen and oxygen. They can also be used directly to compress these gases and to compress air.

We have to move away from the polluting use of fossil fuels to power motor cars, and compressed air is a potential fuel. Air compressed mechanically by windmills could be bottled and distributed to every garage in the country just as petrol is today. We could build the necessary infrastructure just as we did to supply petroleum fuels. Compressed air bottles could be exchanged on an empty-for-full basis at any garage. The same is true for hydrogen. Hydrogen burned in an internal or external combustion engine would produce water as the product of combustion. Oxygen, the other product of electrolysis, would find other industrial uses.

## Water Power

Water is a non-polluting power source. The technology is well understood and could soon be up and running at a fraction of the cost of nuclear power. If we took all the billions required to build a nuclear power plant and all the billions required to decommission it (and we still do not have a satisfactory way of dealing with nuclear waste), then the money would be available to take on a plethora of people-friendly ways of producing electricity. These schemes would last a lifetime and we could enjoy cheap, reliable electricity. Low-technology solutions are more sustainable and can be more easily distributed throughout the country.

# Chapter IV

---

*Alienation*

People need diversity in their lives. Increasingly we are becoming units of production rather than deciding for ourselves our direction of travel. We are increasingly being controlled by those who do not care about us because the profit motive is their raison d'être.

Large companies use the internet to ensure that advertisements encourage us to buy because they need consumers. They try to find out what our interests are so that we may become better consumers. It seems that they penetrate our thoughts, our likes and dislikes, without our co-operation in an attempt to manipulate our thinking. From our past patterns of spending, they get to know us better than we know ourselves. The more we consume, the more they find out about us. Their intrusion becomes sinister, but it is we who are colluding to give them the information with which they can control our behaviour. There is plenty we can do to put this right.

The billions of profit made by some internet companies does not seem to be reflected in the working conditions of their workforce or their contribution to the exchequer, and so they do not contribute to the provision of the infrastructure on which they rely. To them, workers and consumers are a cheap renewable resource. Because of our fondness for online shopping we are allowing ourselves to be driven into a low-wage, low-productivity economy. Think before you click!

If consumers could pause before they clicked and perhaps not click at all there would be less pollution and a more caring and thoughtful society. If we shopped in towns, town centres would recover their vitality, people would have employment, and society would be reinvigorated. In large food stores we can ensure that people retain their jobs by not using self-service tills. Robots do not need food! Robots do not always enhance our lives; they replace people, and people matter.

There are those who say we cannot go back in time. Indeed in the past people have too often come second to profits. Industry has so often been uncaring about the welfare of its workers, who have lived with inadequate housing, inadequate diets and inadequate healthcare. We can, if we choose, move into a better future, a future fit for people. When people are treated well and feel that society cares about their welfare, everyone will feel a part of a lifestyle that is inclusive and even exciting. If we carry on with more of the same, work will become repetitive and we will feel irrelevant and disposable.

The consumer is in control and we can consume less to have a more compassionate and thoughtful society. Customers are more important to companies than shareholders.

## The Wrong Kind of Production

Cars have become an essential part of our lives. It was previously thought that diesel cars were cleaner than petrol cars, but now we have realised that all fossil fuels pollute the environment and we have to move to alternative fuels. Electric cars may well replace fossil fuel driven vehicles, but there are many possibilities for propulsion, and in any case the whole infrastructure of petrol stations will have to be reconfigured. Electric points can be installed throughout the country, but garages can still be delivery points if the fuel used is hydrogen or compressed air.

Batteries are heavy, need to be recharged and increasingly depend on scarce resources in their construction. Electric motors are also heavy. Hydrogen can be compressed using windmill technology and Stirling engines with low energy input have been demonstrated propelling boats. We must make more effort to find alternative renewable power sources for vehicle propulsion.

Cars themselves have to change. At the moment they are increasingly made so that their workings are inaccessible. High-tech cars made by robots are difficult to repair and maintain without specialist equipment. Cars, like everything else, will have to be made so that they last a lifetime. With the co-operation of manufacturers, garage mechanics could have access to spare parts. Those who manufacture the cars could also be involved with their repair and maintenance. Second-hand cars could be as good as new.

We need caring ecological economics to replace irresponsible capitalism where profit is the only motive. Change has to take place, otherwise pollution will increase, not decrease. Only when public transport is transformed, accessible and affordable will we be coaxed out of our cars. There must be adequate car parking at stations to allow us to leave our cars and continue our journey by train, just as we now have park and ride facilities out of town so that our journeys can be continued by bus.

Formula 1 should be replaced by a race for non-polluting cars so that the best engineers can focus their energy and ingenuity on new technologies, as they have done for Formula E cars. Cars run on fossil fuels can no longer be seen as glamorous; they belong to the past.

We must invest in eco-friendly technology. The old way of mass production using large quantities of raw materials and production lines turning out ever-increasing numbers of cars with built-in obsolescence is not sustainable. In short, we need to develop simpler solutions on tried and tested practice which protect and conserve our finite resources.

## The Problem of Tyres

Tyres cannot yet be recycled. They are a serious problem. Three billion tyres will be manufactured this year, and the number is growing. Three billion tyres a year will be thrown away. Three billion tyres placed side by side would stretch thirty times around the earth.

Bus, lorry and aeroplane tyres are built to be retreaded. We used to retread car tyres, but cheap imports have made it unprofitable to carry out this process. We could make satisfactory, safe and good-performance tyres for retreading, and this would use only one third of the rubber required to make a new tyre.

Rubber trees are a renewable resource, but they eat into the equatorial forests, and so it seems a sensible idea to reduce our need for rubber. Another source of latex has been found in the root of a certain kind of dandelion plant. Indeed the flower produces the same amount of latex from the same area as a rubber tree. A wonderful discovery to have a good source of latex which grows in temperate climates.

If we can make tyres last longer by using cars less, we could begin to reduce the number of tyres produced. There may also be ways of devulcanising tyres using sulphur-digesting microbes. Then it would be possible to reuse the rubber to make more tyres and create a cyclical process.

We have to solve this tyre problem and export the newfound technology so that other countries can recycle also. There has never been a greater need for engineers and scientists to solve these problems. Tyre dumps can be found throughout the countryside full of tyres waiting to be recycled. It is an inconvenient and as yet insurmountable problem. Turning out ever more cars is not a solution. The cost of recycling has to be considered, but the cost of not doing so is unthinkable.

## Aviation: Cities in the Sky

The number of large airliners in the sky at any one time creates as much pollution as a city. In every city airport there's a queue of planes waiting to take off and land all the time, and the direction of travel is for this traffic to grow. It would help if we could fly less and use the train more, since train travel is increasingly powered by electricity and electricity is increasingly produced from renewable resources. Planes could be smaller and we could fly fewer of them. Like Norway we could find new ways to propel our aircraft, but aviation has a long way to go. It would help the planet if we chose to travel on holiday by other means. Railway travel could give just as much pleasure. In every sphere of living we could be more thoughtful about the planet and its needs.

We should not open more runways because by doing so we increase the amount of air travel and more transport will be needed to convey people to and from the airport. Also a large piece of valuable land will be concreted over and people will lose their homes at a time when there is a shortage of houses. There is a promise from the government to plant more trees throughout the country; there is also a desire to concrete over more of the countryside for airports, railways and business sites. Their actions contradict their declared good intentions. Green politics should support green agendas, but as yet there is no consistent criticism of cities in the sky. This just seems to be a fact of life about which we can do nothing. When new runways are built people are compensated and their lives treated as inconsequential, but land is increasingly precious, and people and their homes do matter. We should build more homes, not demolish them.

The climate is changing and increasingly temperatures of 40°C have been recorded in our favourite holiday resorts. We have to reduce our propensity to travel by air to ensure that the planet can recover and allow those who live in these intemperate zones to survive.

We all share the desire to survive, and our chances are diminishing. We have to prioritise our behaviour to change the unhealthy situation for the better. We cannot wait for governments and industry to change their policies; we have to change them by our actions.

To help the environment we could travel to destinations closer to home. Our harbours and fishing ports have been run-down of late, but they could have a new lease of life. Lagoons in Swansea and elsewhere would make our rather neglected seaside towns popular again, just as piers in Hastings and Brighton make these towns wonderful places in which to relax. We could do so much to make Britain the best holiday destination for the British.

## Trains

With high-speed trains the emphasis on speed is forcing the pace all the time, when what we need is more gracious travel. Train carriages used to be aesthetically pleasing; different woods were used in the construction of coaches where we now use plastics, and people were treated like celebrities. How much more enjoyable rail travel could be! Instead of standing for the duration of a journey we could put on more coaches and make the service more luxurious. We could bring back the Brighton Belle and compete on comfort rather than speed. The focus has to be on improving existing services. Tickets should purchase a seat on a train. Trains do not need to be fast, but they do need to be on time. We could coax people out of their cars by making trains the best way to travel long distances. We have to be more thoughtful to save the planet and ourselves.

## Shipping

Shipping, whether cruise ships or container ships, is a major cause of pollution. One giant container ship produces as much pollution as 50 million cars. Vessels have grown in size and cruise liners no longer look like the old ships, such as the *Queen Mary*, which were graceful and elegant. Instead they look like floating multi-storey car parks. They are crammed with as many people as possible to maximise profit.

Little thought seems to be given to pollution at sea. Ship building used to be a major industry in Britain. Now the ship building is carried out by countries which can supply cheap labour and undercut prices.

Technology is changing, and Norway is leading the way in hybrid propulsion systems which significantly reduce pollution. In Orkney engineers have found a way to use surplus tidal and wind energy to produce hydrogen by electrolysis. Developing hydrogen fuel cell technology will require investment in infrastructure and financial support. We have to develop a future moving away from fossil fuels and towards less polluting (or, in the case of hydrogen, non-polluting) fuels.

Ships should shrink in size so that they can take to the seas without damaging the oceans and the planet. We have to learn to sail on the oceans without contaminating them at all. We have to build ships smaller for a new age.

Smaller vessels could be built around the British coast by British craftsmen. It used to be a major industry and could be again. Shipbuilding is essential for an island nation and an island people. We have to show the way by designing ships that use wind, solar energy, and fuel cells for propulsion. We can also ensure that shipbuilders are taken better care of and properly remunerated so that they can afford to travel on their creations.

Shipbuilding companies have to take care of people and the planet, and it is not possible to do one without the other. We cannot relax until we have the possibility of 100% employment and everyone is employed in a real job.

When people are more careful about their consumption, perhaps the need for container ships will diminish and they could also be reduced in size. We have to find ways to travel without damaging the planet.

# CHAPTER V

_Banking_

In this current society, where the profit motive trumps even security, bankers have become avaricious. Some bankers have completely undermined the banking system because they cared only about profit and survival even at the customer's expense. They have acted like carpetbaggers and put their customers at risk. They now have a reputation to recover and this will only happen when they put people first. It used to be the case that the bank manager was a trusted figure, a pillar of the community, whose advice customers could feel had their interest at heart. When you put money in a bank you need to know that it will be safe and that the bank cares.

Banks can encourage businesses which develop eco-technology and should discourage large asset strippers whose only concern is to make a profit. Some of our unique companies which develop products of benefit to our society are sold for profit to a foreign country. We should be more protective of our creativity and inventions.

When bankers invest our money it should be in ecologically friendly ways that will enhance the lives of everyone in society and contribute to the wellbeing of the planet. They could encourage and invest in companies that reuse scrap metal, companies that try to substitute biodegradable materials for plastic, and companies that promote the non-polluting fuels of the future. The food industry, farming, fishing and all associated industries are worthy of our support. Pollution is damaging our oceans, our atmosphere and our land; we have to ensure that our money invested will be used in ecologically responsible ways by people at the top who make it their business to care about our planet and its people.

Ethical banking should be the direction of all banks. Banks have to be available in a community so that businesses can deposit takings and withdraw money with ease. Everyone in a community needs personal banking because money is still the main means of exchange. The recent trend is for bank branches to close because increasingly people are banking through the internet, but there must be a choice if we care about people. Many people are not on the internet, and furthermore the internet has been seen not to be people-friendly. The internet increases the risk of fraud and identity theft, and those of us who wish to avoid internet banking have valid reasons for doing so. Ethical banking has to be community banking so that everyone has access to their money when it is required.

## Valued for Life

Large buses which are powered by fossil fuels travel round the country nearly empty. Electric buses could be smaller but more numerous to provide a service in remote areas. Inadequate transport creates isolation and dependency.

In a more caring society people could contribute for longer if we did away with the idea of forced retirement and redundancy. People are increasingly being made redundant at an early age, but without a growing population our skills would be needed for longer. In a society where people are valued, the health of the nation would undoubtedly improve. If people's talents and skills could be valued and utilised whilst adapting to different needs as we get older, then we could feel that we had a lifetime's involvement in society.

Our society is ageist. It makes getting old a disease, and older citizens are retired and made to feel unwanted when they are at the peak of their careers. Ageism creates despondency; it makes people feel like spare parts on the debit side of the equation, and no longer of value. The elderly have invaluable experience and are just the people to encourage the young to acquire skills so that they may develop their interests to the full.

Many elderly would much rather repair and reuse faulty equipment than replace it and fit in more to an age where built-in obsolescence is increasingly undesirable. They do not often purchase on a whim and they would much rather shop in town than 'click to put it in the basket'. It is the elderly who could support the new age of ecological economics and ethical banking.

## Hospitals

Hospitals are part of care in the community. Community hospitals should provide emergency care so that people do not have far to travel for help. Local community hospitals can provide respite care and recovery care so that those who have had serious problems with their health have time to recover before they return home. Ultrasound and X-ray equipment should be available so that problems can be diagnosed and dealt with in the community where possible. This would enable the city hospital to deal with stabilising critical conditions effectively.

The problem with centralising care is that staff have to relocate to an area where care is delivered in a hospital and leave remote areas without nurses, doctors and twenty-four-hour care in the community. Governments should be ensuring that young people can work in their communities if they would prefer. It seems that wherever you look there is no thought given to the choices open to young people for jobs in the future. Increasingly skills will migrate to large urban areas, leaving remote areas with impoverished facilities.

In remote areas the first concern of ambulance crews is to get patients to the nearest hospital within 'the golden hour'. The amount of driving they have to do should be minimised. Large hospitals need small community hospitals to support them. Having to drive miles to and from a hospital can't be the best option.

Continual referral to large and remote facilities is to be avoided, especially when local hospitals could have the capability to provide treatment and observation and to stabilise a seriously ill patient before moving to a specialist facility. Travelling in the new ecological age should be reduced to a minimum. People matter and people support the infrastructure.

## Parks

Parks are still beautiful areas in cities. They are the lungs of the city, and all green areas should be treasured.

Parks used to have bandstands and music was enjoyed on warm sunny days. Many parks had lakes where young and old could sail model boats. They are wonderful places for recreation, encouraging bowling and tennis. We are now so concerned that someone may come to harm near water that ponds are filled in and hobbies are not encouraged enough. We should cater for everyone's interests and take some risks to make life worth living.

When youngsters do not have access to parks and creative activities then they are at a loose end and really put in danger. The rising crime rate points to a lack of supervision and care in the lives of young people when they feel excluded.

The Parks Department grows flowers in abundance to adorn a city. What better way to enhance a city than with a profusion of flowers? City gardens encourage insects, and seats in parks enable the thoughtful to relax and enjoy the green spaces and the activities of others. City parks are so important for the wellbeing of the city, from the carbon dioxide that they absorb to the fresh air they generate for the people who live nearby and enjoy them.

## Allotments

Allotments encourage self-sufficiency and also provide, for anyone who has rented one, a very satisfying and rewarding pastime. We are concerned that the public should keep fit. Gardening is therapeutic and provides necessary exercise. More land should be set aside for allotments because people need to keep in touch with the countryside. Allotments provide activity in which the whole family can engage and an introduction to a career in horticulture.

# CHAPTER VI

_____

## Ethics

We may think of ethics as a subject studied at university and out of reach of the rest of the population, yet ethical considerations are involved in everything we do. Together we create the ethos of our society; it can be harsh or caring, cruel or kind. The culture of a society sets the standards to which people are expected to conform, but cultures do change over time, for better or worse. Sometimes changes happen so gradually that we may be unaware of them, yet they can have devastating effects on our lives and become categorised as inconvenient realities.

This book holds that there is a new imperative for change: it's called survival. There has to be a new ethos which is more caring and thoughtful because everything is related. In this book we use the term _ethical_ to describe behaviour that is characterised by a care for the planet and its inhabitants. Ethics and ecology go hand in hand.

Forty percent of insects have been wiped out by fertilisers and climate change. We have to think of this as more than an inconvenient reality; it is a threat and a tragedy. Losing biodiversity at this rate is not acceptable. We really will have to travel in a different direction to create a different ethos and a different future.

When using scarce and renewable resources a company hopes to make a profit. Profit will be greater if the use of scarce resources is minimised and these resources recycled wherever possible. Renewable resources have to be replaced so that the production process does not deplete them and is sustainable, as natural processes are. We have to ensure that profit is returned to the cycle and not taken out of use. The culture must change so that when a profit is made everyone can benefit in perpetuity.

Profit is essential in any business to pay for the costs, including wages, of running it; it can also be employed in creating an ethos that is caring and kind. If maximising profit becomes the overriding goal, however, costs will be cut, people will become an undesirable expense and the service will be diminished, harsh, and cruel.

## Priorities

People have been talking about saving the planet for many years, but we have reached a stage where it may be too late if we don't do something about it very soon. It was thought that governments would take on board all the ecological issues, but they definitely have not. They say they care about people and the planet but then make decisions which negate their pronouncements.

We always have to ask what our priorities are. Do we want top-down decisions in favour of maximising profits or do we want decent work for everyone in an inclusive society? Do we want to have trains packed like sardines and manned only by a driver, or driverless trains, to maximise profits, or do we want a community on wheels? We could be served by railway staff who could provide services on the train while it is travelling so that we could arrive at our destination safe, refreshed, and ready for work.

Why do away with ticket offices at stations if it is not just to save money? What about those who supplied the tickets and helped us on our way? We are not all on the internet and we need to be assisted when we are unaccustomed to the system. We are not all London commuters. Some of us need guards because we need assistance getting on a train.

During the Olympic Games in London it was helpful citizens who made the Games a success. We need people and people need work. We cannot be written off and dismissed as expenses. People matter.

## Propaganda

The government uses propaganda to promote the status quo. This is the way things have always been. The government promotes growth, the market economy, maximisation of profits, and consumerism around the world, and seeks cheap labour abroad when costs rise at home. Governments want us to think that it is they who deliver change that will protect the environment, but so far they have achieved very little.

It does not seem to matter which party is in control. They each have their policies but so far have not promoted ecological economics when it conflicts with the maximisation of profits. Growth is desired because they insist that it is growth which creates prosperity. This seems so far from the reality faced by so many people who are undoubtedly suffering because there are fewer and fewer real jobs available. People have become an unjustifiable expense that reduces opportunities for profit maximisation. This is a culture of indifference. We all seem to be on zero-hour contracts because we are all dispensable. At any time businesses can be moved to areas where labour is cheaper.

If everyone were valued and involved in making society and the world a better place then this would be real success. The wealth that is produced by utilising the planet's resources could be more evenly distributed providing a decent job for everyone. The leaders of business should stay in touch with their workers, otherwise there will be exploitation.

This culture where we accept the unacceptable as the norm is founded in propaganda. This has been the norm for a very long time. Many of us have good lives and nice homes, but not everyone. Society should not accept that many people do not have nice homes and have to use food banks. This cannot be a norm we live with, because this norm is also destroying the planet, and everything is related. We have to become good stewards of the planet's resources. Some will have to use less to allow others to use more.

I am optimistic that there are many people who care and are thoughtful about how their money is spent. There will always be those who are unethical and arrogant and greedy and will make hay while the sun shines to increase their personal wealth, but this is unacceptable, irresponsible behaviour which is to be frowned upon. The world is in a mess because of such people who care only about their position in society even when around them everything is in chaos.

We have to change the culture. The consumer can be in charge of decision-making, and we can choose which employers to support and try to avoid those who are exploitative by not buying their products. For the planet to continue supporting us we have to support a more ecologically thoughtful way of life. We have to replace greed with moderation. It is we who decide who the heroes who deserve credit are, and we have to find ways to discourage those who are exploitative. This is how the world will change.

## Compartmentalisation

In order to protect the status quo, those in power try to label those who care about the planet as foolish or irresponsible. Such concerned individuals are seen to be inconvenient and pigeonholed as the enemy within. The status quo provides a sense of continuity and we are encouraged not to rock the boat, to leave things as they are, because change is difficult to manage. Any new thinking will be managed by being compartmentalised and dealt with by the full force of the law, as with climate change protesters today, but consumers are difficult to control. When we begin to ignore the continuous advertising that controls how we spend our money, when we focus elsewhere, then we will take control of our spending. Advertising is clearly designed to influence our choices, but as consumers we can take back control by making ethical choices and promoting ecological economics.

Conventional economics is sustaining, maybe widening, social inequalities: the rich are getting richer and the poor are getting poorer. The growth of food banks tells us that many are getting left behind. Exploitation of people and resources inevitably becomes universal and will destroy all life on the planet. We are all waiting for a very different ethos to emerge, a new direction of travel, but this will only come about if everyone behaves responsibly.

## International Development

0.7% of GDP is set aside for international development. Perhaps the money could be used to generate developments which reduce the use of the earth's non-renewable resources and which encourage ecological technologies which will arrest climate change. We need to help farmers to plant vegetation and diverse new crops which will cope with climate change. It is of special interest to farmers in Africa and across the equator to discover ways to manage climate change and reduce temperatures. They have unlimited solar energy to produce electricity and to pump water for irrigation; solar energy can be used to produce fresh water from seawater. They need the technologists, engineers, and specialists to develop their renewable resources to their full advantage. This is why we need to invest in technical colleges, here and abroad, to train the next generation to produce food and energy in our country and around the world.

# CHAPTER VII

---

*Ecological Economics Revisited*

Ideally an ecological approach to economics will prevail. We cannot continue to use the planet's resources to maximise output. Growth and profit allow only a few to become wealthy at the planet's expense. We need a more compassionate economics which will redistribute the resources we have at our disposal carefully and more equably.

We have to consider the interrelatedness of life on the planet. If the thoughtless exploitation of the planet's resources remains normalised, the outcome will be the extinction of species we need for our survival, food banks, destitution, and eventually our own extinction. Destitution cannot become the norm with which we live, especially when there is an alternative. The survival of the fittest could be a race to the bottom where not just the few but the many will be destitute. We have to co-operate to survive. We have to promote moderation rather than greed and generosity rather than exploitation.

Slavery is not just something that happened in our past; it is happening now with zero-hour contracts. It happens when whole workforces are cruelly dismissed after a lifetime of loyalty to enable a company to relocate. People become wage slaves when earned income covers only the bare essentials and there is insufficient income to save for a rainy day. It seems not to be in the employer's interest to make employees self-sufficient. Employees need regular pay to clear debts and it is a serious matter to be unemployed. Employers believe they need wage slaves to ensure a reliable workforce. The need for food banks demonstrates that we have become an uncaring society inured to the suffering of others. Everyone needs a home and time to develop skills and talents.

Care of the planet and its people will only happen when the goodwill of enough customers wrests back control from monopolies and thoughtless employers whose only consideration is profit. Everyone needs to have a home, to have warmth and to be fed. There is still a plentiful supply of resources to give everyone a good life if we use them in moderation. Instead of maximising production we could manufacture products for life and we could recycle all materials to create a society where there is no waste. We could try to export this good practice to save the planet.

Unions are no longer effective in supporting workers' rights because of the global economy. Bad working practices can be transferred from our country elsewhere. In an amoral society it does not matter to distributors or consumers whether goods are made in Britain or by wage slaves elsewhere. Ethical consumption is the ultimate non-violent protest.

## An Amoral Society

Everyone concedes that slavery is wrong, but slavery is as real now as it ever was. When millions of people in a society, through no fault of their own, find themselves destitute, then people are being treated as slaves. Everyone is talented in some way and if we abuse people, society becomes dystopic. People are the country's wealth, the only renewable resource we can provide, but only if we can behave in ways that support the planet and each other.

In an ethical society all work would be directed to the good of the planet and its inhabitants. Too often people have to take employment out of necessity and are in no position to choose how their effort is directed, and very often it is directed to maximise profit for the few.

## Ecological Sciences

We can no longer fiddle while Rome burns. The sciences have to refocus on the health of all life on the planet. Geology, for example, is presently used to assist oil companies to find new deposits to supply industry. Oil is seen as a limitless resource, but this oil has been deposited over millions of years and is irreplaceable. It is one thing to be curious about the structure of the planet, but we cannot destroy it to satisfy that curiosity. We have to use the minimum of resources carefully so that they last another thousand years. We have to leave resources for the generations to come.

Chemists are needed more than ever to discover the processes which will convert plastics and vulcanised rubber to a form which can be reused. Renewable resources like cardboard and cellulose can be reused for packaging of food so that the packaging is more easily recycled. We need cyclical processes. This new focus will direct the future. New processes will provide work in a society which is co-operative, taking into consideration all life on the planet.

If we could reuse plastic there would be less need to use up our precious resources. At the moment recycling is still of secondary importance, an inconvenient reality. We export considerable quantities of waste plastic when we should be exporting the technology to deal with it. Reducing and reusing waste is one of the most important issues in our lifetime.

Psychologists have many uses. They can support industry by helping to sell produce: placing products so that they get noticed and trying to influence the consumer through advertising. On the other hand there are so many neglected and abused children who need counselling so that they can lead useful lives. Often the abusers have been abused in childhood but left to their own devices. The cycle of despair could be ended.

Industry will only function to make the country prosperous when it ceases to be exploitative and if everyone is contributing in a self-sustaining supportive environment.

Philosophy cannot exist in a vacuum. When we are

threatened with extinction, we have to work together to survive. When survival is threatened, every mind has to be focused on undermining the status quo so that we can have a future.

It's unnecessary to establish a colony on Mars. Rockets use too much fuel and too many resources. In time scientists will not need to look at the red planet and wonder about its past because this planet could easily go the same way.

Scientists are now trying to remove debris circling the planet; better it was not put there in the first place. Does it really make for a better world to be able to spy and eavesdrop on each other?

## The Internet

Like the comets in *The Day of the Triffids* the internet has been found to be absorbing, entertaining, a wonderful invention which can solve all our problems, but actually it could become a major problem. The banks wish us to be a society based on internet banking without the infrastructure of banks. Soon all its employees will be in a high office block in London and we'll all have to bank on the internet. Paper money will not need to be made at all because we will be encouraged to use our cards. In fact already some businesses are cashless.

What will happen when the electricity is cut off or the system, for any reason, is not operating? In a cashless society we will all have to hold our breath. We rely on the internet so much that it could be serious if the apps don't work and we find that nothing in the house works either.

This is not the way forward because, like the population in *The Day of the Triffids*, we become increasingly vulnerable. The more we are dazzled by the internet, the more distant we become from the day-to-day functioning of all our basic needs. We become out of touch with our basic necessities and are helpless to keep control of our daily lives. Someone else cleverer than us has to fix it. We become a part of a totalitarian state where a few privileged elite will have the knowhow to turn on the lights while the rest of us wait. Hackers can do damage and, despite reassurances, we can be quite sure that the few scientists in control have not thought of everything, just as the bankers got it so wrong recently. Those in control could 'switch you off' if they disagreed with you. They treat us as if we are stupid when it is they who are out of touch with reality, comfortable in their sense of entitlement. We always have to ask *what if?*

It is essential that paper money is always available as a back-up to electronic money, that solar panels, for example, are able to supply electricity directly should the grid fail for any reason. The country as a whole needs 'fallback' solutions to future problems. Centralisation and control by the few of the internet could see a rather nasty situation develop where those in power supervise our behaviour and we have no privacy. George Orwell wrote about this in his vision of the future, *Nineteen Eighty-Four*.

We are handing all the power and control to a minority who could use their power to make life impossible for everyone else, and possibly ultimately also for themselves. Can we be sure they always have our best interests at heart? Would they know what our best interests were? They show little sign of this even when the planet is under threat. Their first response to discontent is to subdue it, to stop strikes and ensure that workers are never able to dictate terms or even contribute to alleviate their concerns. The miners were, in the words of Margaret Thatcher during the miners' strikes in the 1980s, 'the enemy within'.

When 1% of the people own 50% of the land in this country I see little benevolence there. This is the result of exploitation and control. We have to change from being enthusiastic servants to people who will always ask *what if?* Exploitation and control by those who have no idea how to behave is not a good recipe for the future. The status quo has to change and people everywhere have to force change by changing their pattern of consumption dramatically.

The internet encourages abuse, violence, and discourteous communication. It seems to bring out the worst in people and we are helpless to do anything about it. People on the internet can be selfish too, because they exclude others not on the internet. Society, if we are to survive, should instead become kinder, more considerate, and more tolerant of other preferences.

Banking is unsafe when done on the internet

because it makes fraud and theft more likely. The fact that one person has had his life savings stolen, that one child takes his own life, should give us pause. Such tragedies question an unthinking enthusiasm for such technology. The internet can be used for good or evil. Technology cannot be divorced from ethical behaviour.

# Chapter VIII

*The BBC*

*B*BC could stand for *Biased Broadcasting Corporation* because it's firmly behind big business and the financial markets. It promotes their interests and keeps us up to date with all the news of their successes and failures, their ups and downs, without asking whether there might just be an alternative point of view.

The BBC is London-centric and the news from the North is rarely commented upon, as if London produced the only news of interest to the nation. The BBC has a duty to report matters of national interest impartially. The wealth of a nation should be invested throughout the nation in a way that recognises that regional interests and national interests are not separate things; all people have the same needs wherever they are. The country will be more successful if infrastructure is invested in throughout the country, not just in a few areas.

The rise of regional broadcasting which purports to represent an alternative perspective is a reaction to a perceived arrogant London-centric bias. The present discontent in large areas of the land is the result of institutionalised neglect over a long period, and this schism is aggravated by an organisation which is increasingly seen as illiberal, out of touch, and comfortable in the conviction of its own entitlement.

The presentation of news on the BBC is rapid and repetitive, too often against a background of unnecessary, or even irrelevant, music. Presenters, it seems, are trained to talk without pause between news items or even sentences. The reason for the slick performance is not apparent and the experience is not pleasant. After half an hour of rushing through the news that the BBC thinks is important to the nation it starts all over again. The same half-hour of news is given throughout the day.

Opinions are limited to the thoughts of politicians and newscasters, and often opposing points of view are not given consideration; news becomes propaganda. Those who supported Brexit, for instance, have been disdained and frozen out of the conversation altogether. The BBC is in danger of becoming the establishment point of view and its public service role vitiated.

## Pensions

The pension age is rising all the time because there is less money being set aside for pensions. In fact a state pension can only be paid to those who are retiring by those who are currently working. In other words it is a Ponzi scheme. Ponzi schemes are illegal in any other business. More effort should be made by government to reserve greater sums of money to fund state pensions so that we can work to provide our own pensions during our working lives.

It seems unfair that a man who labours outdoors all his life should retire at the same age as one who has an office job. Not all work requires the same energy and effort, and therefore one cannot expect a labourer to be as fit at sixty as someone who has had lighter work. Some acknowledgement has to be made of the variety of work that people undertake. Teachers and nurses would find it hard to work until they are seventy and so more consideration should be given to the health of employees.

So much money is being hidden from Her Majesty's Revenue and Customs, not by employees but by those who harvest money from their businesses. Every owner of a business has the right to a reasonable salary. An employer who accepted such a salary would gain the respect of everyone in the community. Unfortunately many employers seek wealth to gain respect. They hire lawyers and experts to avoid tax and if necessary take their profits out of the country. These profits are made by everyone in the company, and so removing assets to enrich the few is undermining the whole community. It is these assets which could provide holidays, a decent living, and early retirement for the workers. The goal when making cars, for example, should not be to maximise production to enrich employers but to create a work–life balance.

At the moment too much money is leaving the country and pensions are starved of funds. Employees have to work until they drop, except politicians, because they formulate all the rules and do not see the injustice of the system. They seem blind to the fact that some people do two jobs to barely survive and many families have two breadwinners who are still unable to make ends meet. There may be full employment, but, although people are working hard, they are treated with contempt when they ask for assistance. Universal Credit should not be necessary in a nation where there is full employment and where everyone has a right to useful work in an inclusive, caring society. All workers have to be decently paid. We cannot feel good about paying minimum wages and creating destitution.

Growth is unsustainable. If the population could be stabilised, the production of all goods could gradually be reduced to save resources. The repair and reuse of equipment could be a healthy and productive activity, saving even more resources for future generations. New ethical products can be exported, but so also should the new technology and philosophy so that all countries can be encouraged to co-operate to reduce the human footprint rather than to compete. This is not a choice but a necessity of enlightened self-interest.

## An Unchristian Society

The government supports the status quo. It promotes financial services at the expense of manufacturing. Accumulating wealth is seen as a worthwhile endeavour and favours the few who are honoured and esteemed. This implies that those who find it impossible to make ends meet can be ignored or regarded as lazy because they are unsuccessful.

The rich think their wealth insulates them from catastrophe. They move around the world acting like philanthropists, providing mosquito nets and water, while the earth is being destroyed by their selfish actions. They are like litter pickers tackling the problem from the wrong end, causing the climate to change by their selfishness and disregard for the future. These ruthless exploiters, whether of crops or minerals or people, do not care about the third world or any world because they are so detached from reality.

This is not a Christian society. It is thought that slavery has been abolished, but it still exists, hidden by indifference and vested interest. Governments favour projects like HS2, developments at Heathrow Airport, and nuclear power, which take money from the many and give to the few. We make appropriating the earth's resources an honourable enterprise, but this is theft on a large scale; the poor are penalised for doing the same thing on a small scale. We could honour those who turn up for essential work that is poorly paid. Carers and cleaners are the heroes and should be paid properly. Ruthless behaviour should be discouraged and is not worthy of our esteem.

Religions everywhere respond to the competitive status quo by being divisive, insisting that the ritual is more important than the message. Within Islam and

Christianity there are competing views. Following the rituals makes you an adherent while the message is sidelined. Religions fiddle while Rome burns. Each belief system thinks it has to compete to survive and the common message for humanity is lost.

We have to refocus on saving the planet and generating better human relationships. When exploitation and the maximisation of profit are the drivers for all enterprises, people and the planet will be diminished and everyone endangered. Religion must not promote competition and avarice but should instead promote co-operation and the welfare of all in an inclusive society. We should spend our money judiciously to effect change in society. We have to be self-sufficient, using our changing pattern of consumption to save the planet's resources, and assist other countries to do the same. We have to lead by example. A fair society is preferable to a charitable society.

## A Climate of Change, Not Climate Change

During the Second World War, manufacturers were most adaptable and found that they could alter production processes to help the war effort. It's not nearly so challenging to evolve products which do not end up on the council tip. Making products for life should be a comparatively easy direction to take; in fact, who would turn away from a product with a lifetime guarantee? Such a product would be worth paying a little more for, especially if maintenance, fitting and collection were also part of the service, Furthermore the product could also be made in Britain by British workers.

What faces us now is more serious than wars between countries because the climate is changing and making life difficult for millions of people. It's only a matter of time before it affects us.

Not only are we making the wrong kinds of cars, but we are also eating the wrong kinds of food and obesity is a problem. We grow an enormous variety of vegetables in this country, which are nutritious and plentiful. This is not a time of scarcity as it was after the war. We are having to adapt in a time of plenty, but, just as after the war we ensured that everyone was fed by issuing ration books, so today we have to ensure that food is shared out so that no one starves. It should be possible today to house and feed everyone.

The world cannot support an ever-growing population. Climate change will drive population movement, putting greater pressure on the resources of more favoured areas. This combination of increasing population and shrinking resources will overcome our best endeavours if we fail to resolve its causes. When a country goes to the expense of training its own key workers like doctors and nurses, and when the population is experiencing the problems of climate change, we should not solve our own problems by recruiting abroad. In this country growing the population to promote consumerism only satisfies the owners of industry who are entrapped by the need to grow profits and enlarge production at the expense of everything else. Growth and consumerism engender exploitation. Consumers should keep the car longer, get it repaired, and cut down on consumption. Consumers are in control and really can effect change.

During the war we faced an existential threat and we adapted to survive; today we face an existential threat from climate change and population growth resulting from our exploitation of the planet, and we must adapt again. We cannot wait until we have damaged the planet so much that there is no going back and we find ourselves in an impossible situation. The decisions we make now will determine the world's future.

Controlling consumerism is a part of the solution and everyone will have to take part in the struggle to survive. We are already carefully considering the purchases we make as we try to reduce our use of plastic. Governments will take action when consumers demand that more emphasis be put on environmental issues. What is needed is a change of culture; limiting consumption is the ultimate non-violent protest.

# Conclusion

There has been growing concern of late about climate change, its implications for us and, significantly, the effect of human activities on it. It's the new imperative, though these concerns go back at least to the 1970s.

There is evidence that climate change has occurred throughout the history of the earth. The difference now is that we are not only conscious of it and its potentially catastrophic effects for us, but are, with a growing awareness of our possible part in it, less inclined to be fatalistic about the outcomes.

Much less debatable is that we live on a finite planet with finite resources which we are using up at a growing rate, and that we are accumulating problems of waste disposal that are reaching alarming proportions. For much of this waste there is no natural restorative. Autumn leaves will wither and return their atoms to the earth because there exist unseen, and for most of us unknown, legions of fungi and microscopic lifeforms working tirelessly to bring this about; this has not been the case for plastic waste. Although radioactive fission occurs naturally, our only answer to the 'disposal' of radioactive material from our industrial activities is to bury it in concrete. This is not a new solution, of course; the thermal energy of the earth itself is buried under the earth's crust, to be released from time to time with devastating effect by volcanic action. The difference is that nature doesn't care about the consequences; we must.

Human society is dominated by the old economics evolved when the world was a 'bigger' place, when the teeming masses could be transported or recruited to populate 'new worlds' of 'limitless' opportunity and riches, when people were hierarchically regimented, when the vast majority of them could be regarded as the resources of the few, and when a few could police the world. It was a time of enterprise, of 'wealth creation', when collateral costs were viewed as inconsequential. This book contends that wealth cannot be 'created' and the attendant costs have not been inconsequential.

We are where we are; we cannot go back, and, even though many of us may be better off than our forebears, we cannot go on unchanged. Things need to change, but our belief systems, our social structures, our institutions are built to resist change.

The driver of the old economics is consumerism through mass production, economies of scale, the creation of demand. We have been engaged in a race to keep the roundabout turning; we need to slow the roundabout while avoiding the crash of a too-sudden deceleration. We must do this to make time for alternatives to be developed. We have to wean ourselves off increasing consumption, increasing growth, increasing obsolescence, increasing waste, and increasing depletion of resources. We have to encourage innovation, reduce the burden of legislation, loosen the grip of bureaucracies. Having too many laws and regulations stifles innovation. Much of this we must expect to be the concern of our elected representatives, but as consumers we can all make choices. There is nothing idealistic in these pages; it's a matter of enlightened self-interest.

We are, quite apart from all the conflicts raging across the earth, at war: a war to regain our struggling life support system, and we will need all the resilience which characterised wartime societies. We have to learn to purchase less and value more. We have to learn again to save up for things, to make do and mend, to shop prudently.

It could be liberating; the future could be fun!

Low-tech, low-cost solutions could be developed where we now employ highly sophisticated and specialised high-cost technologies which lock us into the old economics, drive up growth, and accelerate the roundabout we need to get off.

There's nothing retrograde or unprecedented about this. Windmills were established technology in ancient Crete; modern windmills are direct descendants.

Wars have shown us how adaptable and innovative we can be. We have turned our ploughshares into swords and we have turned them back again. We have used the technology of war to develop the technology of peace.

There's a whole field of alternative non-polluting energy sources to be researched. There's a whole new design philosophy of reusability to be worked out.

We can stop throwing away food before and after it gets to the table. We can learn to deal with our pollution. We can stop wasting our resources. We must look again at our priorities.

We're in a race against time. Perhaps there's not time enough, but it's in everyone's interest to try. If we keep our activities on a human scale, maybe the passengers can regain control of the runaway train.

# BIBLIOGRAPHY

Asimov, A. (1975). *Guide to science, volume 1: The physical sciences*. London: Penguin.

BBC Radio 4. *Costing the earth*.

Dickson, D. (1974). *Alternative technology and the politics of technical change*. London: Fontana.

Dudgeon, P. (2009). *Our Glasgow*. London: Headline

Ehrlich, P, and Harriman, R L. (1971). *How to be a survivor*. New York: Ballantine.

Institution of Engineering and Technology. *E&T magazine*.

Lovelock, J. (2014). *A rough ride to the future*. London: Allen Lane.

Meadows, D, Meadows, D, Randers, J, and Behrens, W. (1972). *The limits to growth*. Washington, DC: Universe.

Owen, D F. (1974). *What is ecology?* Oxford: Oxford University Press.

Pass, C, Lowes, B, and Davies, L. (1999). *Unwin Hyman dictionary of economics*. Leicester: Unwin Hyman.

Shirley, J. (1659). Death the leveller. In Quiller-Couch, A. (1907). *The Oxford book of English verse, 1250–1900*. Oxford: Clarendon.

Sterland, E G. (1964). *Applied heat for national certificate*. London: English Universities Press.

Tressell, R. (1914). *The ragged-trousered philanthropists*. London: Grant Richards.